Symbols of America

LIBERTY BELL

TABLE OF CONTENTS

A Crabtree Seedlings Book

School-to-Home Support for Caregivers and Teachers

This book helps children grow by letting them practice reading. Here are a few guiding questions to help the reader with building his or her comprehension skills. Possible answers appear here in red.

Before Reading:

- What do I think this book is about?
    - *I think this book is about the Liberty Bell.*
    - *I think this book is about when they rang the Liberty Bell.*

- What do I want to learn about this topic?
    - *I want to learn more about how the Liberty Bell was made.*
    - *I want to learn more about the crack in the Liberty Bell.*

During Reading:

- I wonder why...
    - *I wonder why the Liberty Bell is made of mostly copper and tin.*
    - *I wonder why the Liberty Bell was located in Philadelphia, Pennsylvania.*

- What have I learned so far?
    - *I have learned that the original cast for the Liberty Bell was made in London, England.*
    - *I have learned that the message on the bell is "Proclaim liberty throughout all the land."*

After Reading:

- What details did I learn about this topic?
    - *I have learned that the Liberty Bell was rung to mark the signing of the US Constitution.*
    - *I have learned that slavery is the practice of people owning other people.*

- Read the book again and look for the vocabulary words.
    - *I see the word **slavery** on page 8, and the word **copper** on page 14. The other glossary words are on pages 22 and 23.*

LIBERTY BELL

The **Liberty** Bell is a **symbol** of America.

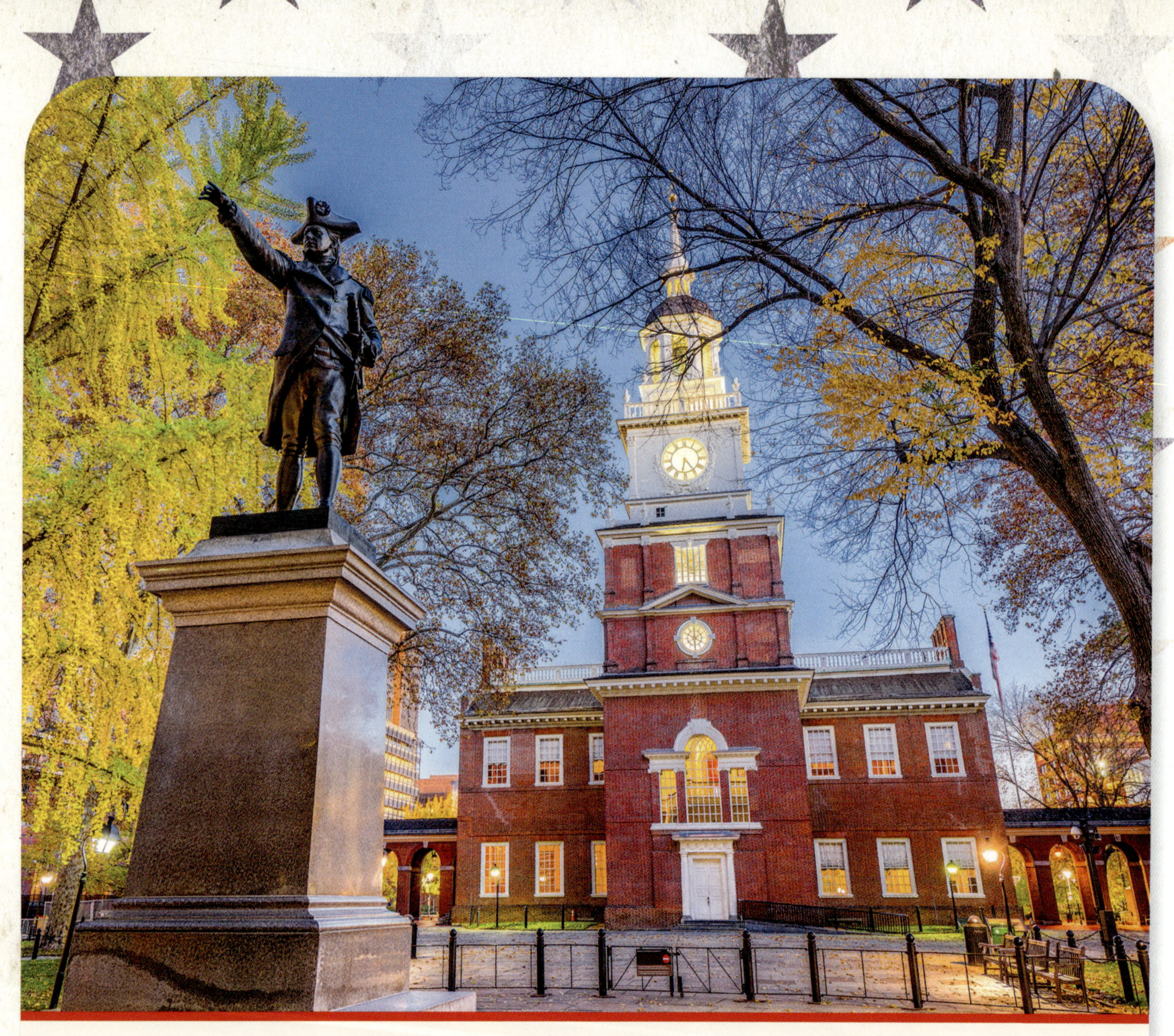

It is located in Philadelphia, Pennsylvania.

It would ring to let people know about events and meetings.

The bell was first in the Pennsylvania State House in 1753. Then it was named the State House Bell.

The original cast was made in London, England.

People fighting to end **slavery** called it the Liberty Bell.

In the late 1800s, the bell traveled to fairs so people could view it.

There is a message on the bell. It says, “Proclaim liberty throughout all the land unto all the inhabitants thereof.”

ALL THE LAND UNTO
OF THE PROVINCE OF

The wooden yoke, or beam, which holds the bell, is made from American elm.

The 1976 **bicentennial** dollar coin has the Liberty Bell.

The Liberty Bell is mostly made of **copper** and tin. It weighs 2,080 lbs (943 kg).

A black rhinoceros weighs about 2,000 lbs (907 kg).

The bell rang in 1787 for the signing of the **constitution**.

It likely did not ring on July 4, 1776, the first Independence Day, as it was under repair.

It was last rung on George Washington's birthday celebration in 1846. This is when the worst crack happened.

The crack was made larger by a repair called “stop drilling.”

Many people visit Liberty Bell Center to see the Liberty Bell.

They are proud to see this important symbol of America.

Glossary

bicentennial (bai-sen-TEH-nee-uhl): Two hundred years

constitution (KON-sti-too-shun): A document that describes the laws and beliefs of a country

copper (KAA-pr): A red-brown metal

liberty (LI-br-tee): Being free without unfair restrictions

slavery (SLAY-vr-ee): The practice of people owning other people

symbol (SIM-bl): A thing that represents something else

Index

About the Author

Christina Earley lives in sunny South Florida with her husband and son. She enjoys traveling around the United States and learning about different historical places. Her hobbies include hiking, yoga, and baking.

Written by: Christina Earley
Designed by: Kathy Walsh
Proofreader: Petrice Custance

Photographs: Shutterstock: cover: ©Edwin Verin; ©MT511, ©dz; Title Pg: ©MT511, ©dz; Pg 4-21 ©MT511; Pg 3 & 23: ©Dan Mall on Unsplash; Pg 4: ©Sean Pavone; Pg 5 @Library of Congress; Pg 6: @Wiki; Pg 7: ©peiyang; Pg 8, 23 ©Everett Collection; Pg 9: @Library of Congress; Pg 11: ©Martin Conyon; Pg 12: ©Tony Rice; Pg 13, 23 ©jlgeranis; Pg 14, 22 ©Dario Lo Presti; Pg 14: ©rsooll; Pg 15: ©Conservation Photojournalism; Pg 16, 22 @Wiki; Pg 18: Everett Collection; Pg 19: Martin Conyon; Pg 20 ©Roman Babakin

Library and Archives Canada Cataloguing in Publication
CIP available at Library and Archives Canada

Library of Congress Cataloging-in-Publication Data
CIP available at Library of Congress

Crabtree Publishing Company
www.crabtreebooks.com 1-800-387-7650

Printed in the U.S.A./072022/CG20220201

Published in the United States
Crabtree Publishing
347 Fifth Avenue, Suite 1402-145
New York, NY, 10016

Published in Canada
Crabtree Publishing
616 Welland Ave.
St. Catharines, Ontario L2M 5V6